Author:

Jacqueline Morley studied English literature at Oxford University. She has taught English and history and now works as a freelance writer. She has written historical fiction and non-fiction for children.

Artist:

David Antram was born in Brighton, England, in 1958. He studied at Eastbourne College of Art and then worked in advertising for 15 years before becoming a full-time artist. He has illustrated many children's non-fiction books.

Series creator:

David Salariya was born in Dundee, Scotland. He has illustrated a wide range of books and has created and designed many new series for publishers in the UK and overseas. David established The Salariya Book Company in 1989. He lives in Brighton with his wife, illustrator Shirley Willis, and their son, Jonathan.

Editor: **Stephen Haynes**

Editorial Assistant: **Mark Williams**

Visit our **new** online shop at
shop.salariya.com
for great offers, gift ideas, all our new releases and free postage and packaging.

Published in Great Britain in MMXIII by Book House, an imprint of
The Salariya Book Company Ltd
25 Marlborough Place, Brighton BN1 1UB
www.salariya.com
www.book-house.co.uk

PB ISBN-13: 978-1-908973-32-0

SALARIYA

1 3 5 7 9 8 6 4 2

A CIP catalogue record for this book is available from the British Library.

Printed and bound in China.

Visit our website at **www.book-house.co.uk** or go to **www.salariya.com** for **free** electronic versions of:
You Wouldn't Want to be an Egyptian Mummy!
You Wouldn't Want to be a Roman Gladiator!
You Wouldn't Want to be a Polar Explorer!
You Wouldn't Want to sail on a 19th-Century Whaling Ship!

PAPER FROM SUSTAINABLE FORESTS

Avoid meeting Typhoid Mary!

Written by
Jacqueline Morley

Illustrated by
David Antram

Created and designed by
David Salariya

The Danger Zone™

BOOK HOUSE

Contents

Introduction

I t's 20 June 1909. You're a New York journalist flipping through the Sunday papers over breakfast to see what your rivals have to say. In the *New York American* you find a sensational article about a deadly disease.

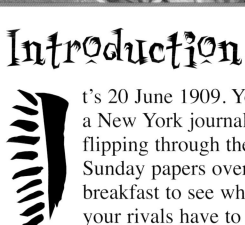

'TYPHOID MARY'
Extraordinary Trail of Death and Disease

MARY MALLON, an apparently healthy New York cook, has been found to be breeding deadly typhoid fever germs inside her digestive tract. She sheds them wherever she works. The food she dishes up is fatal. Yet Mary denies that she is responsible for the frequent typhoid cases in families where she has worked as a cook. To protect the public, the New York Health Authority is keeping her prisoner in an isolation hospital – perhaps for life – though she is not guilty of any crime and has not broken the law.

Death in the Kitchen!

IF THIS STORY IS TRUE, you'd certainly want to avoid meeting 'Typhoid Mary' – the thought of it puts you off your breakfast. The paper is calling her the most dangerous woman in America. Yet you can't believe she's really such a monster. This gives you an idea for an article: 'Typhoid Mary, the Truth Behind the Headlines'. What's the real story of the woman they call Typhoid Mary?

Typhoid fever is a disease spread by bacteria in water or food. It causes high fever and severe diarrhoea. Some victims die of dehydration (loss of water from the body) or other complications.

5

A really good cook

First you interview city banker Charles Warren. 'In 1906', he tells you, 'we rented a holiday house on Long Island and hired servants locally. Mary Mallon came to us as cook. She was a good one. Her ice cream, mixed with fresh peaches,* was a winner. She left about three weeks after we got typhoid fever. Happily, none of us died.'

You wonder: Did Mary go because she knew she was to blame? But if so, why didn't she leave at once?

Cooking kills most germs, but raw, unwashed food such as fresh fruit can carry them.

> I hope they like it!

Mary's career

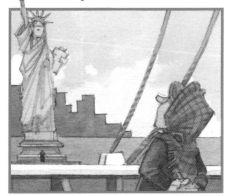

MARY won't discuss her past. You know only that she was born in Ireland in 1869 and came to the United States, alone and barely 15 years old, to find work.

SHE HAD NO TRAINING and took various low-paid jobs, until eventually she persuaded an employment agency that she could cook.

SHE'S BEEN COOKING for wealthy New York families for years now, so the Warrens were quite happy to take her on. She seems to be in excellent health.

Handy hint

If you have a good cook at home, take her on holiday with you instead of hiring a cook when you get to your destination.

This dye will show whether water from the toilet gets into the drinking water.

Fever strikes

THE FIRST PERSON to fall ill is the Warrens' younger daughter, Margaret. The doctor diagnoses typhoid fever.

SOON Margaret's mother, sister, two of the maids and the gardener show the same symptoms: soaring temperature, low pulse rate, nosebleed, nausea and diarrhoea.

WITH NO TYPHOID FEVER anywhere else on Long Island, the source of infection must be in the house. Experts check the drains but find nothing wrong.

Tracing the culprit

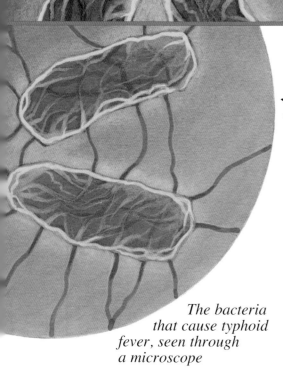

The bacteria that cause typhoid fever, seen through a microscope

Next you visit sanitary engineer George Soper. 'The house had been given the all clear,' he tells you, 'so I checked on the people. Any newcomers around that time? "We had a new cook," the Warrens said. That was the clue! New research shows that some people are "carriers" of a disease – they go on breeding germs long after they've got over the illness. They may not even know they've had it. To see if Mary was a carrier, I traced her job history through employment agency records.'

Bacteria: The new enemy

TYPHOID FEVER is claiming over 35,000 lives a year in the United States at this time. For centuries it was believed that such diseases were caused by 'bad air' created by dirty living conditions.

BY THE 1880s, scientists in France and Germany had proved that many diseases, including typhoid fever, are caused by bacteria – tiny living organisms passed from person to person in water and uncooked food.

PUBLIC HEALTH AUTHORITIES have been given the power to isolate people with dangerous diseases from people who are healthy – by force if necessary.

SOPER FINDS that in the last ten years, typhoid fever occurred in at least seven households in which Mary Mallon was cook.

9

A hot reception

'Before I could report Mary to the authorities,' Soper explains, 'I needed proof that she was breeding bacteria. I found she was cooking for some people called Bowen, so I called on her with what I thought was a reasonable request. I told her I needed to take samples of her blood, urine and faeces to test them for signs of bacteria. She refused to listen! She seemed to think I was making disgusting suggestions and accusing her of a crime. She flew into a rage and went for me with a carving fork.'

You wonder: If Soper had been more tactful, might Mary have listened to what he had to say?

And don't come here again!

Crash!

Tremble

Handy hint

If your job involves asking awkward questions, be prepared for some awkward answers.

A home visit

WITH A COLLEAGUE to back him up, Soper tries again at Mary's lodgings. They have to climb a lot of stairs, and at the top they get a very hostile reception.

THEY LEAVE in a hurry and are followed by violent swearing from the top of the stairs.

11

A woman's touch

'I reported Mary to the New York City Health Authority,' Soper tells you. 'The sanitary inspector thought she might listen to a woman, so he sent his assistant, Dr Sara Josephine Baker, to the Bowens' house. Mary was totally uncooperative, so Dr Baker returned the next day with five police officers and an ambulance. Mary was on the lookout with the carving fork. There was a scuffle on the doorstep, and by the time they got in Mary had disappeared.'

My goodness!

Handy hint

If you know you're not welcome, put your foot in the door when it opens.

After Dr Baker's failed first attempt to see Mary, her boss gets tough with her.

What can we do? There are only five of us.

Get specimens or get her to the hospital!

Anxious to get results, Dr Baker searches the entire house. The servants are no help. They say they know nothing.

13

A scrap of cloth

'I couldn't believe it,' says Dr Baker when you ask her about that day. 'Mary had completely vanished. We spent five hours searching every nook and cranny of the Bowens' house and the house next door. The servants would say nothing. They were obviously taking Mary's side against interfering officials and the police.

'Finally, one of the policemen spotted a tiny scrap of blue calico caught in the door of the closet under the front steps. We hadn't looked inside there before, because there was a whole stack of overflowing dustbins piled against the door. The servants must have stacked them up there once Mary was inside. She came out fighting and yelling. She was very good at both.'

FOOTPRINTS IN THE SNOW lead the police to a chair set up near the fence separating the Bowens' property from next door's. This prompts them to search the next-door house as well.

It's part of a woman's dress!

I've done nothing wrong! I've never had typhoid in my life!

Handy hint
When you've looked for someone in all the possible places, try the impossible ones.

It's like being in a cage with an angry lion.

IT TAKES several policemen to get Mary into the ambulance. Dr Baker then has to sit on her for the whole journey.

15

What the tests showed

Next you interview the superintendent of Willard Parker Hospital, where Mary was taken. 'Tests proved her insides were teeming with bacteria,' he tells you. 'We tried giving her medicines to stop it, but nothing worked. In fact, we tried so many that she probably thought we didn't know what we were doing.

'When we suggested removing her gall bladder, it was the last straw for her. She wouldn't allow it.' You wonder: If they'd concentrated less on zapping bacteria and more on talking things over with Mary, might she have co-operated?

SOPER TELLS MARY in the hospital that if she answers his questions they can publish a book on her case. He'll write it and she'll get the profits.

WITHOUT A WORD, Mary glares at him, pulls her dressing gown around her, goes into the bathroom and slams the door in his face.

One little snip and it's over.

Never!

Handy hint

If you're asked to agree to something you don't see the point of, it's probably safest to say no.

SPECIAL DIETS, together with laxatives, brewer's yeast and urotropin (to sterilise urine), are tried on Mary without any success.

MARY IS A GIFT to scientific research. The hospital tests her blood, urine and faeces regularly to study how a carrier's bacteria production varies.

Isolated!

'Mary wouldn't see reason. She insisted she was a healthy woman, had never had typhoid fever, and couldn't possibly pass it on. So what could we do?' the superintendent asks. 'We have to protect the public, and with that sort of attitude she was a threat to everyone's health. So we sent her to Riverside Isolation Hospital.'

Riverside Hospital is on North Brother Island in New York's East River, opposite the Bronx. Its patients have no means of getting away. Most of them suffer from tuberculosis and hope to leave when they're better, but there is no such hope for Mary. She is housed apart from them in a cabin by the river, with only a fox terrier to keep her company.

FROM HER WINDOW Mary watches the ferry taking lucky patients back to the mainland – and freedom.

MARY IS ALLOWED to mix with hospital staff and to help out with chores that do not involve cooking or handling food.

A NURSE hints that Mary might be freed if she promises to go to a sister in Connecticut and never return to New York. That way the New York authorities would be rid of her. But Mary has no sister and refuses to lie.

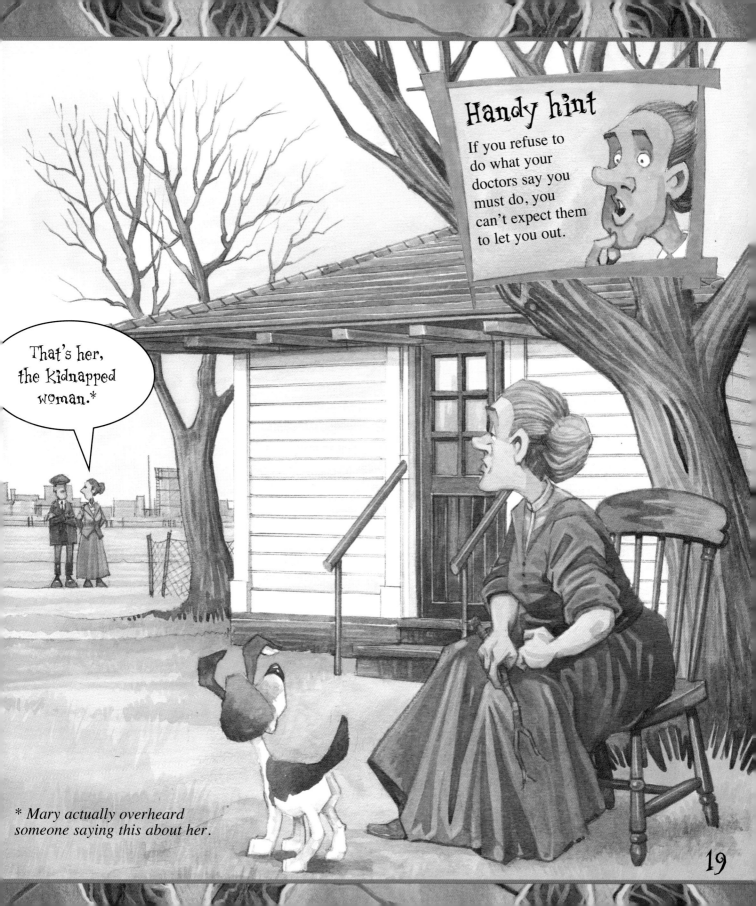

Habeas corpus

If the authorities think they can forget about Mary, they are wrong. In 1909 she starts a legal process known as a writ of 'habeas corpus'.* This is an order saying that a prisoner must be produced in court so that a judge can say whether the imprisonment is lawful.

Mary's case goes to the New York State Supreme Court, and that's why you've just read about her in the newspapers. The judge has accepted the health authority's reasoning and declared Mary's imprisonment lawful. You wonder: The law allows the authorities to detain *sick* persons who endanger the health of others, but Mary is not actually sick. Mary's lawyer did not make that point in court. Would it have made a difference if he had?

A Latin phrase, originating in medieval English law. It means 'You may have the body.'

THE MAIN PROBLEM is Mary's attitude. She will not listen to her doctors' advice, so clearly she cannot be trusted to obey their orders if she is freed.

For and against

MARY'S LAWYER argues that the health authority acted wrongly. It should have let her appeal to a judge before taking away her liberty.

FOR THE PAST YEAR Mary has been smuggling out her own samples of faeces and urine for testing in a private laboratory. The results show no evidence of typhoid fever.

A DOCTOR from the Riverside Hospital testifies that most of Mary's samples swarm with bacteria, but some don't – which explains why some tests have negative results.

ALL THIS PUBLICITY brings Mary a proposal of marriage from a Michigan farmer. She turns him down.

Mary gets a break

Mary is sent back to North Brother Island. But in 1910 her luck changes. A new health commissioner is appointed who thinks Mary has been treated harshly. It's known by now that there are thousands of healthy carriers around. They can't all be locked away. Provided they understand what being a carrier means, and do not cook or handle food, they are not a danger to other people. The commissioner believes Mary has learned her lesson and can now be trusted. Before releasing her he makes sure she has a job to go to. He finds her work as a laundress.

BEFORE ALLOWING MARY to leave the Riverside Isolation Hospital, the health commissioner makes her sign a legal document in which she promises that she will never again work as a cook.

THE COMMISSIONER briefs the press: 'Can't the poor creature be given an opportunity to make a living and have her past forgotten? She is to blame for nothing.'

I miss my old job.

THE HEALTH DEPARTMENT keeps an eye on Mary at first, but after a while she gives them the slip. At the laundry no-one has any idea where she can be found.

23

'Typhoid Mary' strikes again

In 1915 a typhoid outbreak at the Sloane Maternity Hospital in New York affects 25 members of the staff. Two of them die. George Soper and Dr Baker are called in. They learn that the kitchen staff are calling the cook 'Typhoid Mary' – just as a joke, of course. Her name is Mrs Brown. But in the kitchen Dr Baker recognises 'Mrs Brown' at once: It's Mary Mallon.

I know who you are. You're not fooling me!

MEANWHILE, in the superintendent's office, Soper is handed a letter written by 'Mrs Brown'. He recognises Mary's handwriting.

NO SOONER is Mary spotted than she vanishes again. She is traced to the borough of Queens, where a health officer sees a heavily veiled woman carrying a bowl of jelly to a friend – and recognises Mary.

A POLICE SQUAD goes to arrest her. No-one answers the door, so a sergeant pokes his head through an open upper window. He is met with ferocious barking and backs off fast.

Handy hint

If you want to change your identity, go to a place where no-one knows you.

THE SERGEANT comes back with hunks of meat that he tosses into the room. That keeps the dogs busy while the search party creeps past.

THE POLICE go through the house, listening out for Mary as she flees from room to room. They finally corner her in the bathroom.

25

Confined for life

Mary's use of a false name seems to prove that she knows she shouldn't cook and doesn't care what harm she does. You find it difficult to believe that she's as hard-hearted as that – maybe she's convinced the doctors have got it all wrong. But the authorities are taking no chances. They send her back to North Brother Island once and for all.

In time, Mary comes to terms with life there and makes some friends. She's in her fifties when a new young doctor comes to run the hospital laboratory. She gets along well with Mary and hires her as a lab assistant, a job Mary enjoys.

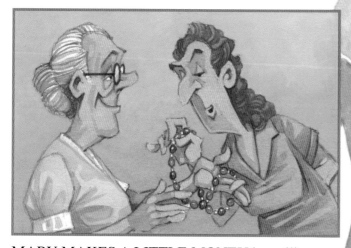

MARY MAKES A LITTLE MONEY by selling her beadwork handicrafts to people on the island.

What would we do without you, Mary?

Handy hint
What can't be cured must be endured. In time, one can get used to anything.

IN THE LAB Mary helps with simple medical tests and general cleaning up.

DURING THE 1920s the authorities start allowing Mary to make day trips to the mainland. She always returns to the island. It has become her home.

Goodbye, Mary

Mary dies on North Brother Island on 11 November 1938, having spent a total of 26 years there. The nine mourners who come to her funeral will not give their names to the press.

You wonder: Was it right to keep her prisoner when thousands of (more co-operative) carriers went free? She wasn't guilty of a crime, only of being pig-headed. The public has to be protected, but Mary had a right to a free life. How far should the human rights of one person be limited for the sake of the rest of us?

That is a question people are still trying to answer today.

IN 1931 Mary is photographed with lab colleague Emma Sherman. Emma says Mary is pleasant to be with, as long as no-one mentions typhoid.

LATE IN LIFE, Mary draws strength from her Roman Catholic faith. The Church's teachings are a great comfort to her.

ON CHRISTMAS MORNING 1932, Mary is paralysed by a stroke. She remains bedridden until her death six years later.

29

Glossary

Bacteria Microscopically small organisms of many types, found almost everywhere. Some types (known as 'germs') cause disease, while other bacteria do useful work, such as breaking down waste matter.

Bronx, the The northernmost of the five boroughs into which New York City is divided.

Calico A cheap cotton material used to make clothing.

Carrier A person who shows no symptoms of a disease but harbours its germs and can infect other people.

Digestive tract The series of organs (throat, stomach, intestines) through which food passes in the process of being digested, and waste products are eliminated.

East River A tidal strait that separates Long Island from the boroughs of Manhattan and the Bronx in New York City.

Faeces The waste product discharged from the bowels after food is digested; excrement.

Gall bladder A small organ below the liver that helps digest fat.

Habeas corpus A legal action through which a person can be released from unlawful imprisonment. It is regarded as the safeguard of individuals from the tyranny of rulers. It was adopted into the United States Constitution from English law.

Isolation hospital A hospital in which patients suffering from infectious diseases are treated. Special precautions are taken to prevent the spread of disease from one person to another.

Long Island A narrow island about 190 km long, lying close to the US mainland and forming part of the state of New York.

New York American A daily newspaper, published from 1901 to

1937, that concentrated on sensational human-interest stories.

North Brother Island An islet in the East River. In the late 19th century it was basically uninhabited. This made it an ideal location for Riverside Hospital, built there in 1885 as a place to isolate dangerously infectious patients. The island is now abandoned and closed to the public.

Public health authorities
Departments of local government which were developed during the 19th century to protect and promote people's health.

Queens A borough of New York City, located at the western end of Long Island.

Sanitary engineer An expert who designs and builds toilets, drains, sewage treatment plants and other facilities to dispose of waste products safely. This helps to reduce the spread of disease.

Specimen A sample of a patient's urine or faeces, which can be tested in a laboratory to find out whether the patient is suffering from, or carrying, a particular disease.

Stroke A loss of brain function caused by a sudden interruption in the blood supply to the brain.

Typhoid fever (often called **typhoid** for short) A dangerous and sometimes fatal disease spread by eating or drinking something contaminated with bacteria from an infected person's faeces. Today, better sanitation and personal hygiene have reduced cases in developed countries, but typhoid fever is still a serious threat worldwide.

Urotropin A powerful antiseptic drug used to treat urinary infections.

Index